EXPLORING COUNTRIES

Afghanistan

by Lisa Owings

BELLWETHER MEDIA • MINNEAPOLIS, MN

Note to Librarians, Teachers, and Parents:

Blastoff! Readers are carefully developed by literacy experts and combine standards-based content with developmentally appropriate text.

Level 1 provides the most support through repetition of high-frequency words, light text, predictable sentence patterns, and strong visual support.

Level 2 offers early readers a bit more challenge through varied simple sentences, increased text load, and less repetition of high-frequency words.

Level 3 advances early-fluent readers toward fluency through increased text and concept load, less reliance on visuals, longer sentences, and more literary language.

Level 4 builds reading stamina by providing more text per page, increased use of punctuation, greater variation in sentence patterns, and increasingly challenging vocabulary.

Level 5 encourages children to move from "learning to read" to "reading to learn" by providing even more text, varied writing styles, and less familiar topics.

Whichever book is right for your reader, Blastoff! Readers are the perfect books to build confidence and encourage a love of reading that will last a lifetime!

This edition first published in 2011 by Bellwether Media, Inc.

No part of this publication may be reproduced in whole or in part without written permission of the publisher. For information regarding permission, write to Bellwether Media, Inc., Attention: Permissions Department, 5357 Penn Avenue South, Minneapolis, MN 55419.

Library of Congress Cataloging-in-Publication Data
Owings, Lisa.
 Afghanistan / by Lisa Owings.
   p. cm. – (Exploring countries) (Blastoff! readers)
 Includes bibliographical references and index.
 Summary: "Developed by literacy experts for students in grades three through seven, this book introduces young readers to the geography and culture of Afghanistan"–Provided by publisher.
 ISBN 978-1-60014-590-2 (hardcover : alk. paper)
 1. Afghanistan–Juvenile literature. I. Title.
 DS351.5.O88 2011
 958.1–dc22   2010040811

Printed in the United States of America, North Mankato, MN.

010111   1176

Contents

Tajikistan

Uzbekistan

Turkmenistan

Kabul ★

Afghanistan

Iran

Pakistan

China

Wakhan
Corridor

Afghanistan is a **landlocked** country in southern Asia. It is nestled in the middle of six other countries and covers 251,827 square miles (652,230 square kilometers). Iran is its neighbor to the west. The Amu Darya River forms part of Afghanistan's northern border with Turkmenistan, Uzbekistan, and Tajikistan. The country shares a long border with Pakistan to the south and east. A narrow strip of land called the Wakhan Corridor touches China in the northeast. Kabul is the capital of Afghanistan. It lies on the Kabul River and is surrounded by mountains.

Mountains cover most of Afghanistan, but the country also has **fertile** plains and rocky deserts. The Hindu Kush mountain range spreads from the northeast to the center of Afghanistan. It then becomes the Baba Mountains. To the west are the Paropamisus Mountains, which slope down to **lowlands** near the border with Iran.

Several rivers flow down from the mountains. These include the Helmand, Kabul, and Hari rivers. The rivers empty into the northern plains. South of the mountains are the dry Rigestan and Margow deserts.

Did you know?

Temperatures in the Afghan deserts often climb to over 100 degrees Fahrenheit (38 degrees Celsius). The extreme heat and lack of water is a deadly combination.

Hari River

Did you know?

Massive earthquakes are common in the Hindu Kush. Thousands of Afghans were injured in major earthquakes in 1998, 2002, and 2005.

The Hindu Kush is the main mountain range in Afghanistan. Many of its peaks reach over 23,000 feet (7,010 meters). The mountaintops are often covered in snow. Forests grow farther down the slopes and in the mountain valleys. The peaks of the Hindu Kush rise near many of Afghanistan's major cities, including Kabul.

The Hindu Kush range is important to the people of Afghanistan. Most of the country's wood is cut from its forests. Its rivers and streams provide Afghanistan with water. The Khyber Pass runs through a southeastern part of the Hindu Kush. This is Afghanistan's main trade route with Pakistan. Every day, hundreds of people travel this road in cars and on camels.

! fun fact

Mount Nowshak is the highest point in Afghanistan. It rises 24,557 feet (7,485 meters) over the Wakhan Corridor.

! fun fact

Markhors roam the mountains of Afghanistan. These wild goats have spiral-shaped horns that can grow over 5 feet (1.5 meters) long!

Many animals live in the landscapes of Afghanistan. Gazelle and foxes race across the plains. In the mountains and forests, wolves and brown bears stalk their prey. The **endangered** snow leopard is hard to spot against white mountain peaks. Only about 150 snow leopards are left in Afghanistan.

bar-headed goose

jerboa

snow leopard

In the deserts, snakes and rodents try to stay cool. The jerboa is a small rodent that is **native** to Afghanistan. It gets most of its water from the food it eats. Birds like the bar-headed goose and the rare Siberian crane **migrate** to Afghanistan's marshes in winter. The marshes are fed by rivers full of brown trout and other fish.

Afghanistan has a **diverse** population of over 29 million people. Pashtuns are the largest group of people. About two out of every five Afghans are Pashtuns. They live by a **code of ethics** called *Pashtunwali*. Pashtuns value honor, courage, and respect. They speak their own language called Pashto.

Tajiks are the second-largest group. Most Tajiks live in the eastern mountains. Other groups in Afghanistan include the Hazaras, Aimaks, Uzbeks, Balochs, and Turkmen. Afghans speak a variety of languages, the most common of which is Dari. Both Pashto and Dari are official languages of Afghanistan.

Speak Dari!

Dari is written in script. However, Dari words can be written in English so you can read them out loud.

English	Dari	How to say it
hello	salaam	sa-LAM
good-bye	khodaa haafez	khoh-DAH HAH-fezz
yes	bale	BAH-leh
no	na	na
please	lotfan	luht-fan
thank you	tashakkor	tah-sha-KOHR
friend	dost	dohst

Today, daily life in Afghanistan is easier than it was under the rule of the **Taliban**. In cities, Afghans walk and bike to get around. People ride buses or taxis. Malls and open-air markets attract shoppers. Some people live in apartments, but most cannot afford them. Instead, they build simple shelters from whatever they can find.

Most Afghans live in the countryside. They have small houses made of brick or stone. Many people rely on camels or donkeys to take them to the nearest town to shop.

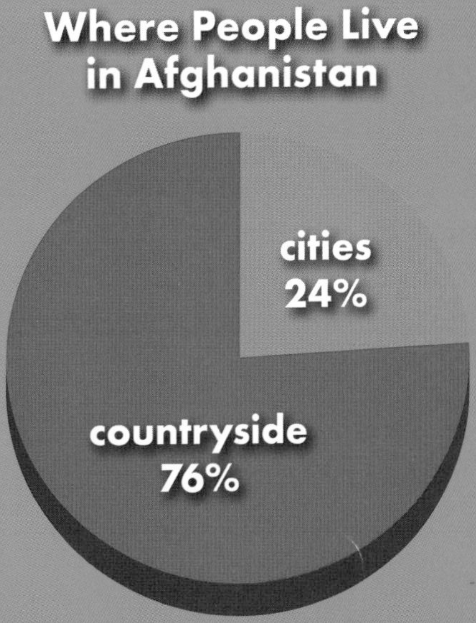

Where People Live in Afghanistan

cities
24%

countryside
76%

Children are required to go to elementary school in Afghanistan. However, many are not able to attend. Damaged buildings and a lack of books, supplies, and teachers keep students out of school. Many children stay home to help their families with work.

Children who do attend elementary school learn to read and write in Dari and Pashto. They study math, social studies, and the religion of Islam. Boys and girls usually attend separate schools. In secondary school, children learn history, science, and Afghan culture. If they graduate, they can apply to universities in Kabul or other major cities.

Where People Work in Afghanistan

farming 79%

services 16%

manufacturing 5%

In the countryside, most Afghans work as farmers or miners. Farmers grow wheat, rice, barley, fruits, nuts, and cotton. They also raise cattle for their meat and milk, and sheep for their wool. Miners collect natural gas, coal, and other **minerals** to send to cities. They also gather gemstones such as emeralds and **lapis lazuli**.

In cities, people work in factories that make clothing, furniture, and other goods. Some people have **service jobs** in shops or restaurants. Others work in construction or as police officers. Many skilled artists weave Afghan carpets. These thick, colorful carpets are famous for their **craftsmanship**.

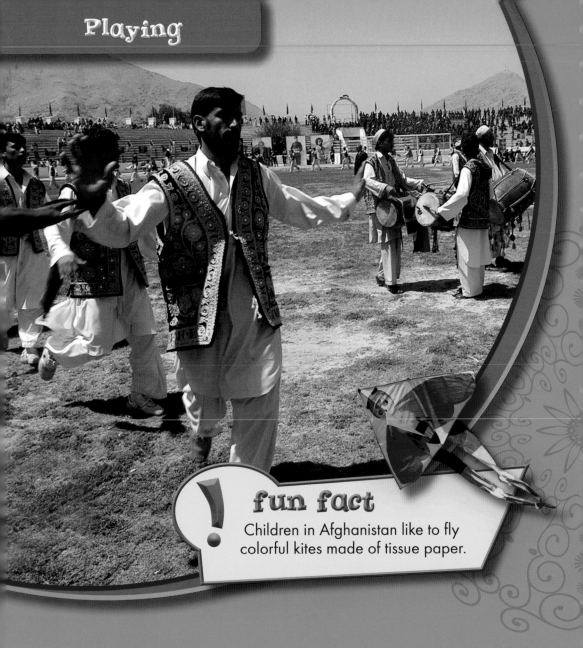

!

fun fact

Children in Afghanistan like to fly colorful kites made of tissue paper.

Afghans love to spend time with friends. Families often talk and drink tea with neighbors. People also enjoy music and dancing. The *attan* is the most popular dance in Afghanistan. The dancers, usually men, form a circle. Their movements get faster and faster in time with the music.

Sports and games are a big part of life in Afghanistan. A traditional sport called *buzkashi* is played on horseback. Riders try to pick up a dead calf or goat and carry it to a goal. The animal sometimes weighs more than 100 pounds (45 kilograms).

buzkashi

Did you know?
Most Afghans do not eat at tables. Instead, they set food out on a carpet on the floor.

Afghans enjoy foods that combine many different flavors. *Pilau* is a mixture of rice, meat, and vegetables seasoned with spices. It is Afghanistan's national dish. Chicken and lamb are favorite meats. They can be grilled or slow-cooked with a variety of flavors. Bread, or *naan*, is served hot from the oven and is often sprinkled with spices.

Instead of silverware, Afghans use *naan* to scoop up their food. For special occasions, dumplings called *khameerbob* are filled with meat or vegetables. Tea is served with every meal. Common desserts include fruits and puddings. *Jalebi*, or fried dough soaked in syrup, is a favorite treat.

! fun fact

Afghans love to share meals with friends. Guests have special seats, and hosts offer them their very best food. Guests try to eat as much as possible to show their thanks!

pilau

jalebi

Nowruz

Most holidays in Afghanistan are Islamic. **Ramadan** is an important holiday for all Muslims. They **fast** from sunrise to sunset every day. Eid al-Fitr celebrates the end of Ramadan. For three days, people feast, give gifts, and play games with family and friends.

Afghans also celebrate many national holidays. August 19 is Independence Day. This is the day in 1919 when Afghanistan gained its independence from the United Kingdom. *Nowruz* is another important holiday. It is the New Year celebration and falls on the first day of spring. Afghans eat traditional foods and watch parades. Many perform **rituals** on *Nowruz* to get rid of bad luck or curses.

! fun fact

Jumping over bonfires is a tradition on *Nowruz*. The fire is thought to burn away sickness and fear. It gives the jumper strength and courage for the new year.

On *Nowruz*, the city of Mazar-e-Sharif fills with thousands of Afghans. They have come to visit the Blue **Mosque**. Its onion-shaped domes tower over a courtyard filled with white doves. The walls of the mosque are covered with blue, yellow, and green **mosaics**.

The Blue Mosque is also called the Shrine of Hazrat Ali. Ali was related to the **Prophet Muhammad**. Many Afghans believe that Ali is buried under the Blue Mosque. This mosque is a place where all Afghans can come together in peace. Many hope that the peace of the mosque will one day spread to all of Afghanistan.

Fast Facts About Afghanistan

Afghanistan's Flag

The Afghan flag has three vertical stripes. The black stripe represents the country's history, the red stands for the blood that was shed in times of war, and the green is hope for the future. In the center of the flag is a white mosque surrounded by other symbols of Islam and Afghanistan. This flag was adopted in 2004.

Official Name: Islamic Republic of Afghanistan

Area: 251,827 square miles (652,230 square kilometers); Afghanistan is the 41st largest country in the world.

Capital City:	Kabul
Important Cities:	Mazar-e-Sharif, Herat, Qandahar, Jalalabad
Population:	29,121,286 (July 2010)
Official Languages:	Dari and Pashto
National Holiday:	Independence Day (August 19)
Religions:	Muslim (99%), Other (1%)
Major Industries:	farming, manufacturing, mining, services
Natural Resources:	natural gas, gemstones, iron ore, copper
Manufactured Products:	textiles, clothing, soap, furniture, cement, chemicals
Farm Products:	wheat, rice, barley, fruits, nuts, dairy products, wool, sheepskins
Unit of Money:	afghani; the afghani is divided into 100 pul.

Glossary

code of ethics—a set of rules for how a person or group should behave

craftsmanship—the skill and artistry with which something is made

diverse—made up of different parts; the Afghan people are diverse because they come from different backgrounds.

endangered—close to becoming extinct

fast—to choose not to eat

fertile—supports growth

landlocked—completely surrounded by land

lapis lazuli—a deep blue gemstone

lowlands—land areas that are lower than the surrounding land

migrate—to move from one place to another, often with the seasons

minerals—elements found in nature; silver, gold, and iron ore are examples of minerals.

mosaics—images or patterns made up of small pieces of colored material; the mosaics on the Blue Mosque are made of painted tiles.

mosque—a building that Muslims use for worship

native—originally from a specific place

Prophet Muhammad—the founder of Islam; Muslims believe Muhammad was a prophet and messenger sent by God.

Ramadan—the ninth month of the Islamic calendar; Ramadan is a time when Muslims fast from sunrise to sunset.

rituals—activities done because of tradition or custom

service jobs—jobs that perform tasks for people or businesses

Taliban—a group of violent Islamic people; the Taliban ruled Afghanistan from 1996 to 2001 and is still fighting for power.

To Learn More

AT THE LIBRARY

Gerber, Larry. *The Taliban in Afghanistan*. New York, N.Y.: Rosen Pub., 2011.

Willis, Terri. *Afghanistan*. New York, N.Y.: Children's Press, 2008.

Winter, Jeanette. *Nasreen's Secret School: A True Story from Afghanistan*. New York, N.Y.: Beach Lane Books, 2009.

ON THE WEB

Learning more about Afghanistan is as easy as 1, 2, 3.

1. Go to www.factsurfer.com.

2. Enter "Afghanistan" into the search box.

3. Click the "Surf" button and you will see a list of related Web sites.

With factsurfer.com, finding more information is just a click away.

Index

The images in this book are reproduced through the courtesy of: Knut Mueller / Photolibrary, front cover; Maisei Raman, front cover (flag), p. 28; Jon Eppard, pp. 4-5; Henry Wilson, pp. 6, 8-9, 11 (top), 23 (bottom), 29; Jane Sweeney / Alamy, p. 7; John Braid, pp. 10-11; Juniors Bildarchiv / Alamy, p. 11 (middle); Don Johnston / Photolibrary, p. 11 (bottom); Jane Sweeney / Photolibrary, pp. 12, 15, 19 (left); Aurora Photos / Alamy, pp. 14, 18; Shehzad Noorani / Photolibrary, pp. 16-17; vario images GmbH & Co. KG / Alamy, p. 19 (right); AFP / Getty Images, pp. 20, 24-25; Ton Koene / Age Fotostock, p. 20 (small); Harald Lueder / Photolibrary, p. 21; Karen Grigoryan, p. 23 (top); Roger Leo / Photolibrary, pp. 26-27; Tischenko Irina, p. 27 (small).